THE PART-TIME SHAMAN HANDBOOK

An Introduction For Beginners

Michael Gillan Maxwell

Copyright © 2015 by MICHAEL GILLAN MAXWELL

PUBLISHED BY UNKNOWN PRESS

First Edition

All rights reserved. This is a work of fiction, all resemblances to persons living or dead are purely coincidental. Nothing may be reproduced without permission of the writer or publisher, unless the work is being quoted in short critical reviews or interviews.

ISBN:9780996352666

edited by Bud Smith
all images by Michael Gillan Maxwell
cover design Bud Smith w/ images by Michael Gillan Maxwell

"But of course, you realize
I'm only a part-time shaman."
—overheard at dinner

for Tonto & Tinkerbell

Contents

7   Opening Incantation

9   Vision Quest

11   Exercise 1
         The Edge
         —*Reflection*

14   Exercise 2
         Day-To-Day
         —*Reflection*

17   Exercise 3
         Community
         —*Reflection*

20   Exercise 4
         Finding Your Way
         —*Reflection*

23   Exercise 5
         Principles For Living
         —*Reflection*

26   Exercise 6
         Things To Do Before Going To Bed
         —*Reflection*

28   Exercise 7
         Health
         —*Reflection*

| 30 | Exercise 8
Observation
—*Reflection* |
|---|---|
| 33 | Exercise 9
The Inner World
—*Reflection* |
| 36 | Exercise 10
Creation
—*Reflection* |
39	Vision Quest
42	It's Not the Fall
44	Closing Incantation
46	Author's Note
47	Money Back Guarantee
50	Appendix I
Part-Time Shaman Starter Kit
52	Appendix II — Suggested Reading
54	Appendix III
Spirit Animals For Beginners
57	Afterword

Opening Incantation

I summon energy from The Six Directions
call upon the radiant angels and spirit guides
Tonto, Twinkle Toes and Tinker Bell
the heebie-jeebies, creepy crawlies
things that go boomp in the night
the spirits of language and radical receptivity
step into the light and guide us
to say the unsayable
speak the unspeakable
know the unknowable
push beyond the safety of outer limits
take our first thought and follow it
down the Byzantine maze
until we no longer recognize it as ours
gaze at things
until they gaze
back at us
gazing back
at them
gazing back
at us.

Vision Quest

These past four days
I watched grass grow
through sun and rain and moon and thunder
not long ago, black walnuts
dropped from the trees
thudding on the earth below
I saw a glossy black racer snake
attacked by swooping birds

These past four days
I watched the creek flow
under the wooden bridge
down the path to the lake
not long ago, I wrote a poem
about a willow tree
branches brushing the ground
limbs bent and gnarly
at the end of the path

These past four days
I watched seasons change
through sun and rain and moon and thunder
not long ago, I saw a groundhog
chase 2 boys, then scurry away
to safety under a porch
I fell to the ground
laughing

Exercise 1 ~ The Edge

Tempt fate
Shoot the rapids in a canoe
Walk under ladders with impunity
Stand knee deep in the roaring surf
Embrace the chaos and fury of thunderstorms

Stare at the sun
Eat Fritos on chili
Purposely step on cracks
Practice archery blindfolded
Tattoo a Celtic shield over your heart

Run with scissors
Stand under a waterfall
Practice walking in the dark
Travel to places you've never been
Do something you're afraid to do

They say we're mostly water. Here I go, sloshing around the corner, tide ebbing and waves rolling. A tsunami in a bathtub. Atlantis and Lemuria lie submerged beneath the ocean of my stomach. Entire aquatic ecosystems evolve into higher life forms inside my liver and spleen. Schools of fish and pods of dolphins gurgle and burble through my blood steam. Sirens summon sailors from the shores of my deep.

Exercise 2 ~ Day-To-Day

Take naps
Daydream
Get out in the sunshine
Look for faces in the clouds
Pay attention to animals that cross your path

Imagine
Listen to birdsong
Breath into your belly
Pay attention to dreams
Feel yourself letting go as you fall asleep

Create your own mythology
Study ancient signs and symbols
Know when to blend into the crowd
Sing harmony with the howling wind
Leave your cell phone in your gym locker

They say we're all here for a reason. When I was a kid I wanted to be a garbage man. Now I take the garbage out every Wednesday night. Finding my purpose is like listening for the sound of one hand clapping in a forest full of popes. Message in my fortune cookie: Wake up, pay attention, celebrate small things.

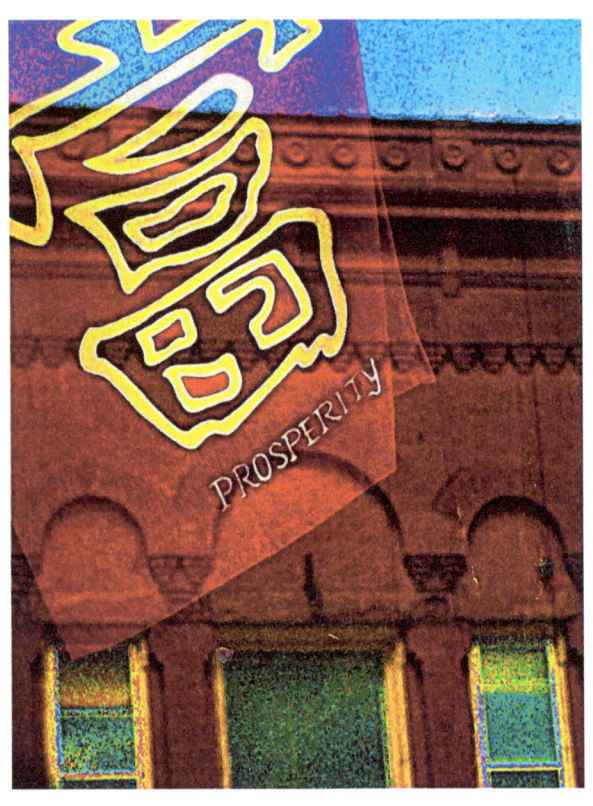

Exercise 3 ~ Community

Kiss and hug
Teach your children goodness
Love your parents unconditionally
Perform service to others every day
Take care of people, pets, plants

Laugh often
Honor tribal elders
Doodle at meetings
Cry when you feel like it
Make music with other people

Don't hold grudges
Get mad and get over it
Commune with your cat
Dialogue with your dog
Sing to birds in their own language

They say we should dance like nobody's watching. Here I am, snowblind and senseless, clomping the fandango in Cuban heels. Up on the table, clicking castanets and circling a vase containing seven tulips the color of bulls' blood; brassy mariachi trumpets blaring to the strumming thunder of a thousand flamenco guitars.

Exercise 4 ~ Finding Your Way

Chase fireflies
Consult the I Ching
Notice the way colors smell
Expect good things to happen
Make offerings to the Four Winds of Change

Listen to loons on a dark lake
Wear white on Spring Equinox
Get out of your mind now and then
Learn all you can from difficult relationships
Project your energy to the Six Horizons

Use fresh spices
Drink water often
Learn to prepare good food
Study medicinal plants and herbs
Learn the Indian names of the full moons

Put more effort into figuring things out, like learning what a hippocampus does or why the hippopotamus is the most dangerous animal in Africa. Come to terms with the fact that One Hour Martinizing is all apple cores and horseshit, and don't you forget it. Even when you feel stuck on the chessboard you still gotta make a move. Get out there, be of service, do something nice for somebody else. Go to Walmart, smile at the cashier. Buy a pencil from a blind man, adopt-a-highway, help a punk rocker cross the road with a chicken stapled to his chest.

Exercise 5 ~ Principles For Living

Shake hands firmly
Belch proudly and smile
Give away your possessions
Don't give away your personal power
Wear blue, green & yellow on Summer Solstice

Be inquisitive
Wear clean underwear
Listen to music as much as possible
Read poetry and write something every day
Don't believe the history you've been taught

Give money away
Honor agreements
Bless the food on your plate
Fart with discretion and respect
Drink the tastiest wine you can afford

My cat does the math, makes the leap from the desk, sticks a four point landing on the fireplace mantel. The Russian and the French judges all award perfect 10s. Compared to that display of elegance and grace, I may as well be a grizzly bear lumbering, tripping across the Aurora Borealis-streaked horizon, top hat in one forepaw, pearl handled walking stick in the other, my enormous hind-quarter paws and claws stuffed into Dixie cups for tap shoes.

Exercise 6 ~ Things To Do Before Going To Bed

Walk down to the lake in a blizzard
Leave poems in public places
Make up your own words
Turn off your cell phone

Make nonsense noises
Chant incantations
Take photographs
Bang on drum
Sing

Dance in the light to the music of the angels
Pay attention to the unexpected
Hear the surf fall on the sand
Smell the earth after the rain
Play the kazoo

I want to play the blues like my hands and heart are on fire. They say you know the secret words to the Music of the Spheres. I can learn the harmony, we can sing together. I'll do my best to understand, even when my heart is filled with impudent judgment and scorn. Be patient. Old dogs learn new tricks slowly.

Exercise 7 ~ Health

Practice Qi Gong outside under a tree
Sleep late when you feel like it
Walk as much as possible
Wear comfortable shoes
Sing in the shower daily

Apply Feng Shui to your living space
Surround yourself with an energy bubble
Drink the best booze you can afford
Play the ukulele
Enjoy food

Start each day with Tai Chi & a sponge bath
Place crystals throughout your house
Recite poetry aloud to your pets
Grow flowers and herbs
Smash your watch

If I listen carefully, the language of forgotten races flows out from spaces between your words. Come with me, I'll show you how to dance naked beneath the sparkling sky. You already know all the steps but remember, sometimes I forget to breathe.

Exercise 8 ~ Observation

Observe behavior of animals as seasons change
Notice the space that surrounds objects
Pay attention to the colors of music
Listen to rain falling at midnight
Draw

Notice what it feels like as you're awakening
Study petroglyphs, and cave paintings
Listen to coyotes late at night
Learn the names of trees
Study animal tracks

Gaze at the night sky from the middle of a lake
Go up on a roof to watch the moon rise
Learn from encounters that annoy you
Listen to spaces between sounds
Take nothing at face value

When we were gypsies, place didn't matter. We made each place our own. We took the things we needed and gave the rest away. We learned first to flinch, then to fight back, and then, to make peace when fighting was no longer necessary.

Exercise 9 ~ The Inner World

Hang mojo objects around your entry ways
Squish your toes in the mud
Play guitar in the dark
Howl at the moon
Practice Reiki

Split firewood from a hundred year old stump
Listen to your heartbeat underwater
Turn hand mirrors face down
Drink only good beer
Learn astrology

Stay up all night on Autumn Equinox
Don't be afraid of the number 13
Walk home at 3 AM
Study numerology
Bless everything

When we were children, time didn't matter. Days went on forever and nights even longer. We learned first to act like adults, then spent the rest of our lives trying to find out way back to being children.

Exercise 10 ~ Creation

Make art from found objects
Learn to use tools
Make a sling shot
Play games
Build stuff

View sunrise at Stonehenge on Winter Solstice
Learn to use your non-dominant hand
You're never too old for balloons
Dance naked in the dark
Draw a new map

Water ski outside of the wake
Color outside the lines
Reinvent yourself
Learn to yodel
Be great

Days glide by, languid as wild swans on a dark lagoon. All the blood and thunder, sound and fury, trials and tribulations; little exorcisms for our souls. Time and place have no hold. We make each place our own.

Vision Quest

She wears a headdress
of jewel encrusted daggers
reflections of this fire and a million fires
that have gone before
flicker in obsidian eyes.

She takes a swig from the bottle
spits it into the fire
flames flare up like a star going supernova
she prods the glowing embers
with a piece of driftwood.

A cataclysm of sparks carried aloft by the wind
whirls like streaking comets
into a sky black as pitch
turning into constellations
and drifting out of sight
her features shift and change in the
shimmering light.

Musky smells of wood smoke and the sea,
eelgrass and dead fish decaying
breakers roll to the shore, churning gravel
and shells in the undertow
I drink from the bottle & choke
down the fiery rum
washing salty brine from my mouth.

Her hair is wild in the updraft
a crown of rainbow serpents
jaguar face as golden as the night
sun of the underworld
she dreams in the languages of star people
her voice, music the color of sapphires.

She sings we are all star born, fallen
from the heavens
grains of sand, tiny specks in a swirling
vortex of cosmic dust
we all have names but return to One
just as raindrops fall like sighs
from the skies into a bottomless ocean.

The fire rages like The Furies, her expression,
fierce and beatific
her eyes, portals to the source of all creation
without another word, she turns and walks to
the water's edge
then wades out
into the thundering surf.

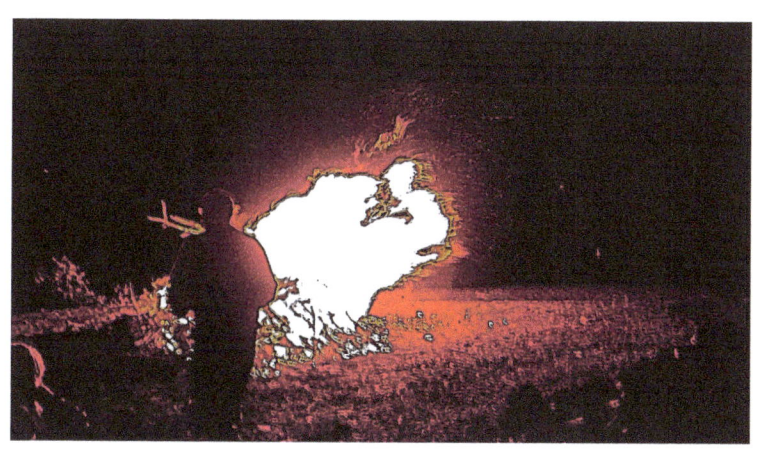

It's Not The Fall

You know
it's going to be a bad day
when you wake up face down
on the pavement

I stumble into the museum
alive on arrival, but bleeding
from cuts and abrasions
after falling in the street
while running to avoid
being hit by a car

the gallery is light and airy
various shades of white
on white on white and pale grays
filtered daylight, late afternoon, early spring
muted footfalls, hushed voices, austere
echoes through translucent chambers

this must be heaven

a place, well lighted and clean
everything made of glass
the seraphim, highest order
of the ninefold angelic hierarchy
harbingers of light and purity
embodied in the form of iPads
reclining on black leather couches
waiting to share the secret key
to the mysteries of the Universe

I should have paid attention
to the shadow
in my peripheral vision
the song of crows, cawing
in the trees
the phantom sound
of someone's voice
whispering a warning

it's not the fall
that kills you
it's the sudden stop

Closing Incantation

I collect beliefs like butterflies
pinned in place, proudly displayed
protected from change.

Spectral forms in shimmering light
images traced in sand with the wind blowing
ephemeral as a desert mirage.

I hold them dear, only to see them go
one by one, until everything I think I know
loses its form and melts back into the ether.

Stark, raving mad from staring into the sun
I loosen the anchors and let them fly
toward every horizon.

Author's Note

The Part-Time Shaman Handbook: An Instruction Manual For Beginners, is written for those who are just beginning their journey. The 10 easy exercises outlined in this manual can be undertaken by just about anyone with an interest in becoming a part-time shaman. Most of the important equipment for starting out is listed in The Part-Time Shaman Starter Kit ~ Appendix 1 at the back of the book.

However, before seriously undertaking explorations into more advanced techniques, certain prerequisites should be met. For those wishing to advance, it is highly recommended that you start by moving to a rustic, unassuming house at the edge of town. You should also practice hanging around dusty bus stations in remote areas, while lurking in shadows with your hat pulled down over your eyes.

Unsupervised experimentation with mind altering substances is not encouraged, especially if you are an air traffic controller or hold the nuclear launch codes for our Civil Defense System. Certainly, no attempt should be made to turn yourself into a jaguar, or even any other animal, for that matter, without first assiduously studying and practicing procedures outlined in *"Shape Shifting For Dummies."*

Money Back Guarantee

If, for any reason, you find the contents of this manual not to your satisfaction, you may receive a full refund by returning the product in its original packaging, accompanied by an incantation and a full description of your most recent vision quest.

Appendix I ~ Part-Time Shaman Starter Kit

Amulet
Bones
Patron Tequila
Bow and arrows
Candles
Carved mask
Cat
Chalk
Deer skull
Dice
Divination cards
Drum
Fire starter
Flute
Gris-gris bag
Guitar
Himalayan salt
I Ching
Incense
Juju charm
Kazoo
Knife
Magic wand
Medicine pouch
Mojo box
Prayer beads
Rattle
Reliquary
St. Christopher medal
Tibetan prayer bell
Ukulele
Walking stick
Wild Turkey feathers
Wizard hat

Appendix II ~ Suggested Reading

Shape Shifting For Dummies

All Things Shaman! Catalogue

So You Want To Be A Shaman?

The Part-Time Shaman Cookbook

Airbnb Destinations For Astral Travelers

Rodeo Clown or Part-Time Shaman? A Memoir

The Ultimate Shape Shifter Trouble Shooting Guide

Appendix III ~ Spirit Animals For Beginners

Cocker Spaniels: Let them run through the underbrush and spoil them with treats.

Crow: Messenger from the Twilight Realm. Pay attention.

Rod Serling: Messenger from the Twilight Zone. Pay CLOSER attention.

Cat: Guardians to the Other World. Lots of issues. Listen up punk!

Iguana: My brother, Danny had a pet iguana named *"Gunga Din."*

Spider: Big Time, GOOD medicine. Don't squash them.

Wildebeest: Pay attention when trekking in the South African bush.

Snake: I know they give everyone the creeps, but they're cool.

Gnome: The most noble of the woodland creatures.

Bear: I'm usually not a hugger but Bear Medicine is all that.

Unicorn: A white horse with a spiral horn. What's not to love?

Afterword

Take a letter to the Poohbah
he'll know what to do.
Ring the mission bell
thank the radiant angels
the answer I seek
has been right here
all along.

Acknowledgements

Special thanks and gratitude to friends, family, beloved pets, writing and art peeps and creative muses, who have influenced and supported my work including, but not limited to:

Ileen Kaplan-Maxwell, Danny Maxwell, Shelley Stahlman, Irving Kaplan, Mark Maxwell, Terry Maxwell, brother Dan Maxwell, Robert Maxwell, Janet Maxwell, Richard Vonier, John Maxwell, Ruth Maxwell, Bud Smith, Robert Vaughan, Bill Yarrow, Meg Tuite, Kathy Fish, Joani Reese, Lawrence Kessenich, John Spence, Carol Spence, Daniel Hoffman, Daniel McLoughlin, Jeff Spence, Lisa Harris, Jane Blumenfeld, Charles Blaney, Jeffrey Teplin, Rudolf Hessberger, Jane Beckmann, Mike Stone, Robert Reuteman, Len Canter, Chris Longwell, Douglas Holtgrewe, Kevin Williams, Rosie, Willsey, Pertie, Saki, Shorty, Brutus, Maggie, Chrissy, Dancy, Chauncy, Ollie, the Beatles, Stones, Bob Dylan and the Dead, Jerry Jeff Walker, Lucinda Williams, Todd Snider, John Prine, Guy Clark, Steve Earl, Miles Davis, Muddy Waters, Robert Rauschenberg, Peter Voulkous, Soji Hamada, Henry Miller, Jack Kerouac, Billy Collins, Jack London, Hunter S. Thompson, everyone who ever hired me or fired me, whoever invented beer, the Radiant Angels, and my spirit guides Tonto and Tinker Bell. If I've somehow left your name off this list ~

I'm sorry, and you're welcome.

About the Author

Michael Gillan Maxwell lives in the Finger Lakes Region of New York where he noodles around with visual art and writes short fiction, poetry, songs, essays, lists, recipes, hybrid weirdness and irate letters to his legislators. His poems and stories have recently appeared in Camroc Press Review, The Santa Fe Literary Review, Uno Kudo, Lost in Thought, Ibbetson Street, Exquisite Duet and a number of other print anthologies and online publications. Michael Gillan Maxwell worked in the trenches reading fiction submissions for JMWW quarterly journal and edited MadHat's Drive-By Book Reviews. A teller of tales and singer of songs, he's prone to random outbursts and may spontaneously combust or break into song at any moment. Maxwell can be found ranting and raving on his website:

Your Own Backyard
www.michaelgillanmaxwell.com

BE YOUR OWN SHAMAN

www.ingramcontent.com/pod-product-compliance
Lightning Source LLC
Chambersburg PA
CBHW041307110426
42743CB00037B/21